Used Cartoons

By Jeff Danziger

Books from
THE CHRISTIAN SCIENCE MONITOR

Political Cartoons from The Christian Science Monitor

For my mother

Books from

THE CHRISTIAN SCIENCE MONITOR ®

A Trick Explained

Some years ago an editor introduced me to a lady at a political confabulation.

"And this is our cartoonist," he said.

The lady's smile froze, then evaporated. My proffered hand dangled expectantly in space.

"You should be ashamed of yourself," she said, and left us summarily.

This incident is mildly instructive. The lady was one of a breed of citizens who take their politics seriously, and to whom I offer an apologia up front. Politics should never be taken seriously, for one simple reason. It's too serious. Take it seriously and you compound the trap. Take it too seriously and there's no way out.

The cartoon is, we hope, an escape. Here among the gray columns of dry reportage and ponderous analysis is something foolishly human. Here someone slips on a banana. If he has any style at all, he'll be laughing as he gets up. If not, somebody help him.

Really effective cartoons are like an ice cube down the back of your shirt. It's meant as a joke, but it's a little too wet and cold to be ignored. It hurts more to get angry than to laugh. Which is why the lady should have shaken hands.

It's an unfair form of criticism, but there's a trick to getting even. Humor is nearly always at someone's expense; a cartoon is hard to rebut. What to do? Write a letter to the editor? Ah, no. And here I betray tightly guarded knowledge. To get even, ask for the original. Say you thought it marvelous! Tell the cartoonist you got a chuckle out of it. You will leave the poor man wondering how he failed.

Not me, of course. I know this trick.

Jeff Danziger

I CAN TYPE.

I CAN SHRED.

I CAN ALTER MEMOS.
I CAN CHANGE DATES,
FAKE LETTERS, AND
SNEAK STUFF OUT OF THE OFFICE.

I WAS HIRED
FOR MY
SKILLS...

DANZIGER

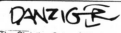

The Christian Science Monitor

Oliver L. North
presents

Oliver North's

FULL MENTAL JACKET

AN O.L. NORTH PRODUCTION
Written by OLIVER L. NORTH based
on a concept by OLIVER NORTH

STARRING OLIVER L. NORTH and STEELHAMMER and BLOOD & GUTS
SCRIPT by OLIVER NORTH • MUSIC by OLIVER NORTH • SPECIAL EFFECTS by O.L. NORTH
with SPECIAL GUEST STAR OLIVER NORTH as the UNKNOWN SOLDIER

NOW PLAYING on a TV NEAR YOU

DANZIGER
The Christian Science Monitor

Dear Col. North,

Thank you for offering to be the "fall guy".

As it turns out that won't be

necessary.

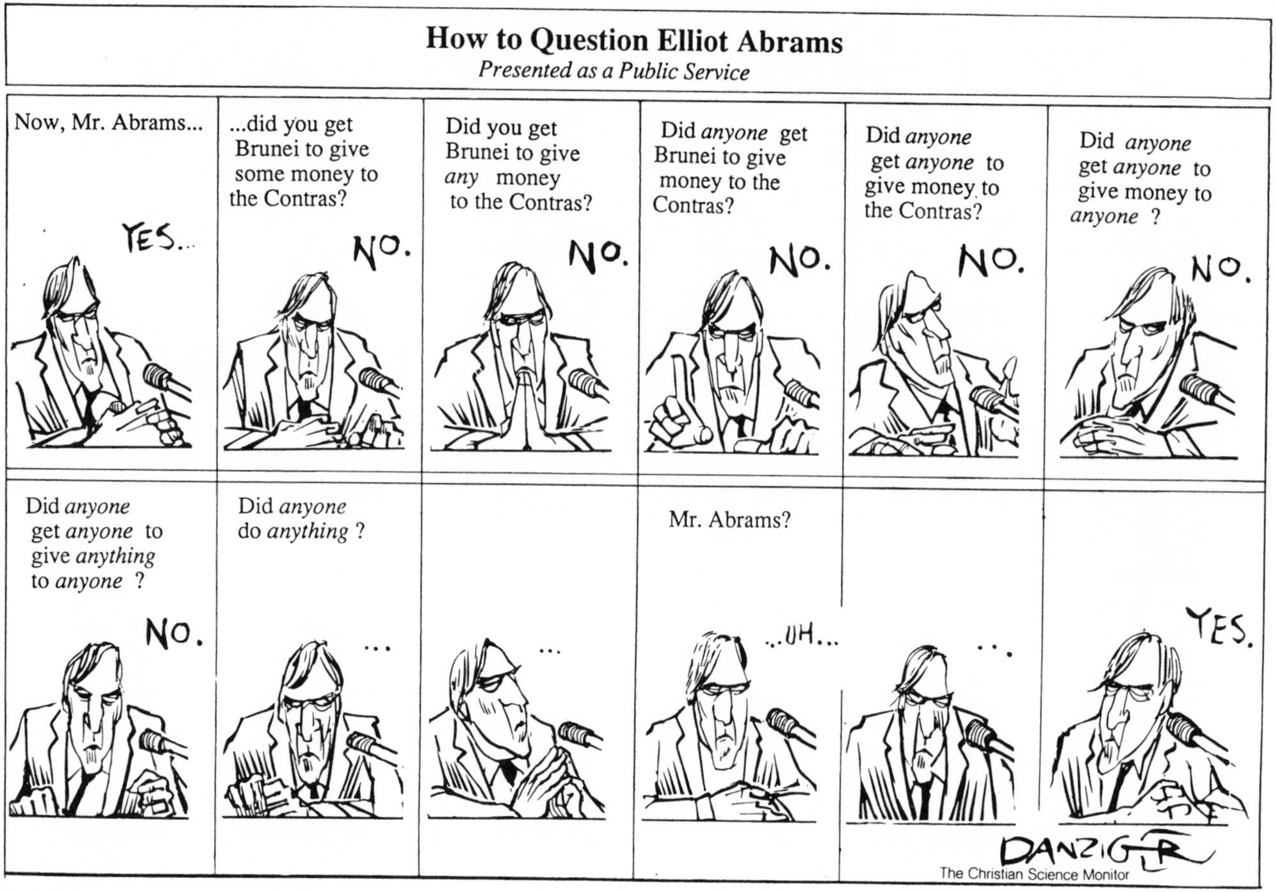
How to Question Elliot Abrams
Presented as a Public Service
Now, Mr. Abrams...
YES...
...did you get Brunei to give some money to the Contras?
NO.
Did you get Brunei to give any money to the Contras?
NO.
Did anyone get Brunei to give money to the Contras?
NO.
Did anyone get anyone to give money to the Contras?
NO.
Did anyone get anyone to give money to anyone ?
NO.
Did anyone get anyone to give anything to anyone ?
NO.
Did anyone do anything ?
...
...
Mr. Abrams?
...UH...
...
YES.
DANZIGER
The Christian Science Monitor

DANZIGER

DANZIGER
The Christian Science Monitor

VOTE

DUVALIER

DANZIGER
The Christian Science Monitor

The Christian Science Monitor

DANZIGER

Iron Fist Policy

The Christian Science Monitor

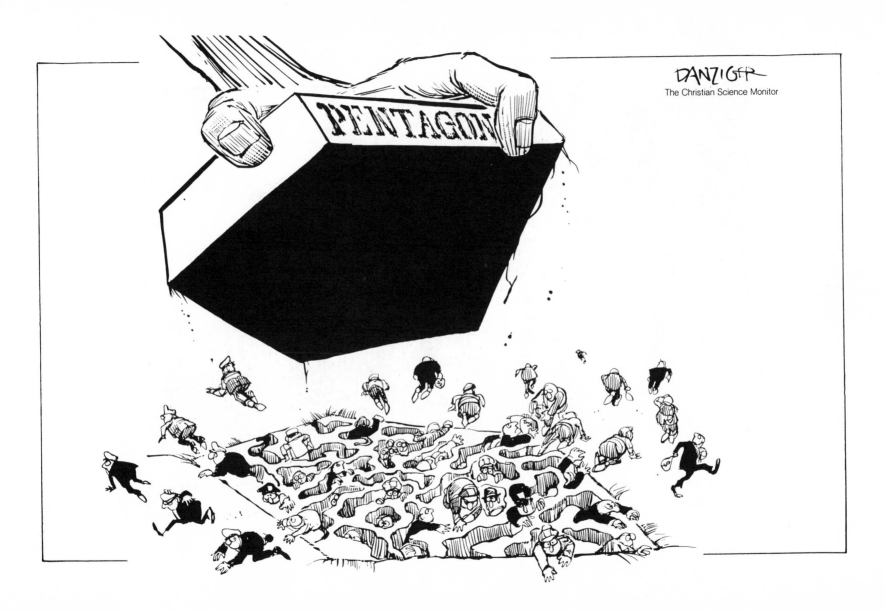

PLEASE RETURN TO WHITE HOUSE PROP. DEPT.

DANZIGER
The Christian Science Monitor

Norman Rockwell   UPDATED RESPECTFULLY BY DANZIGER

DANZIGER
The Christian Science Monitor

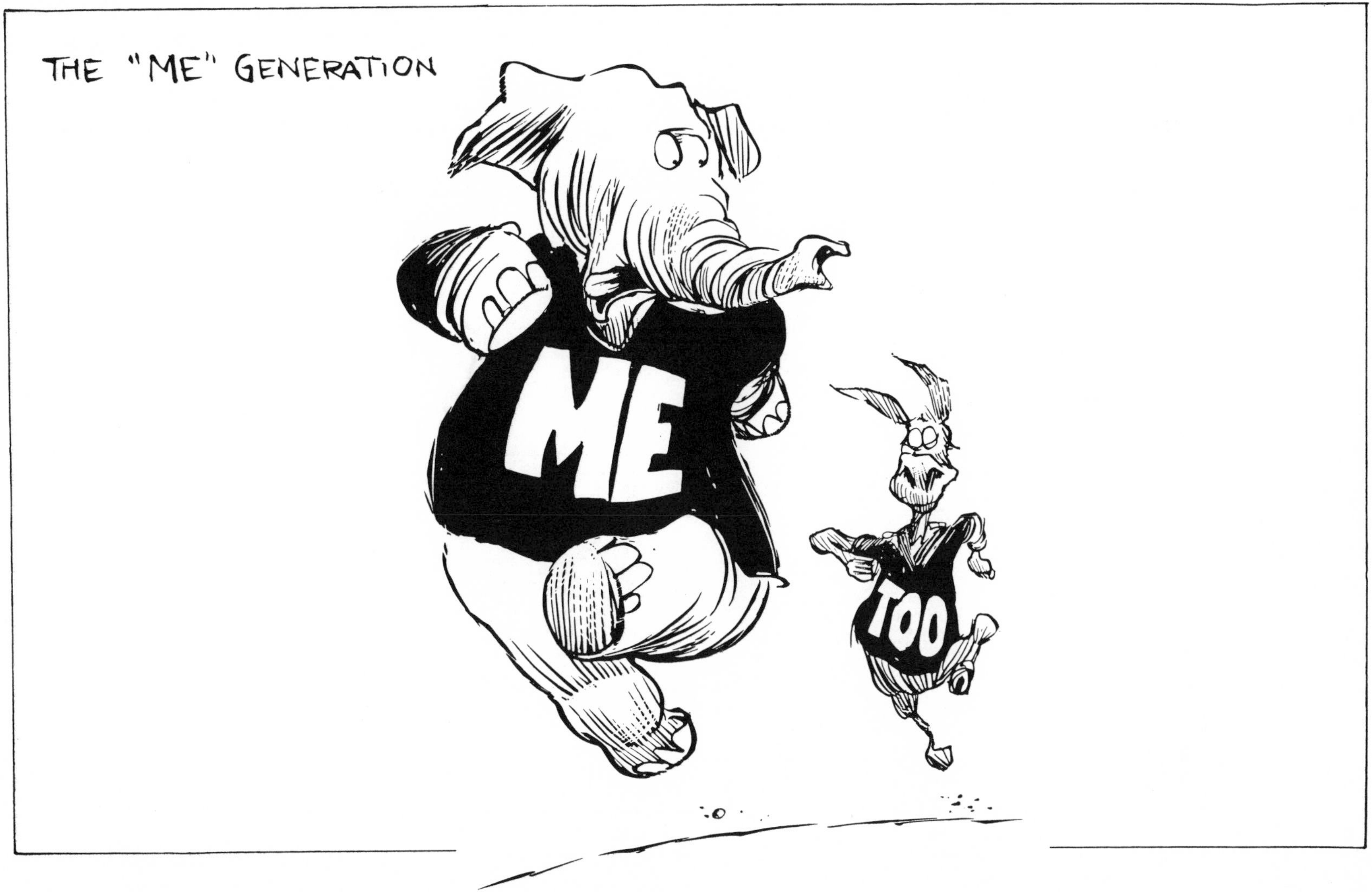
THE "ME" GENERATION
ME
TOO

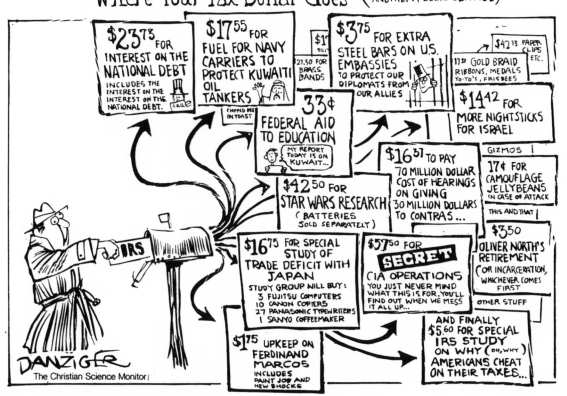

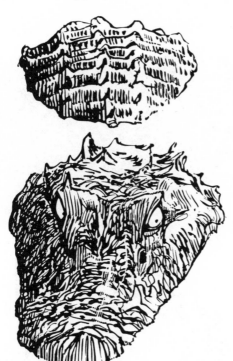

RE-ELECT
AL HAIG

DANZIGER
The Christian Science Monitor

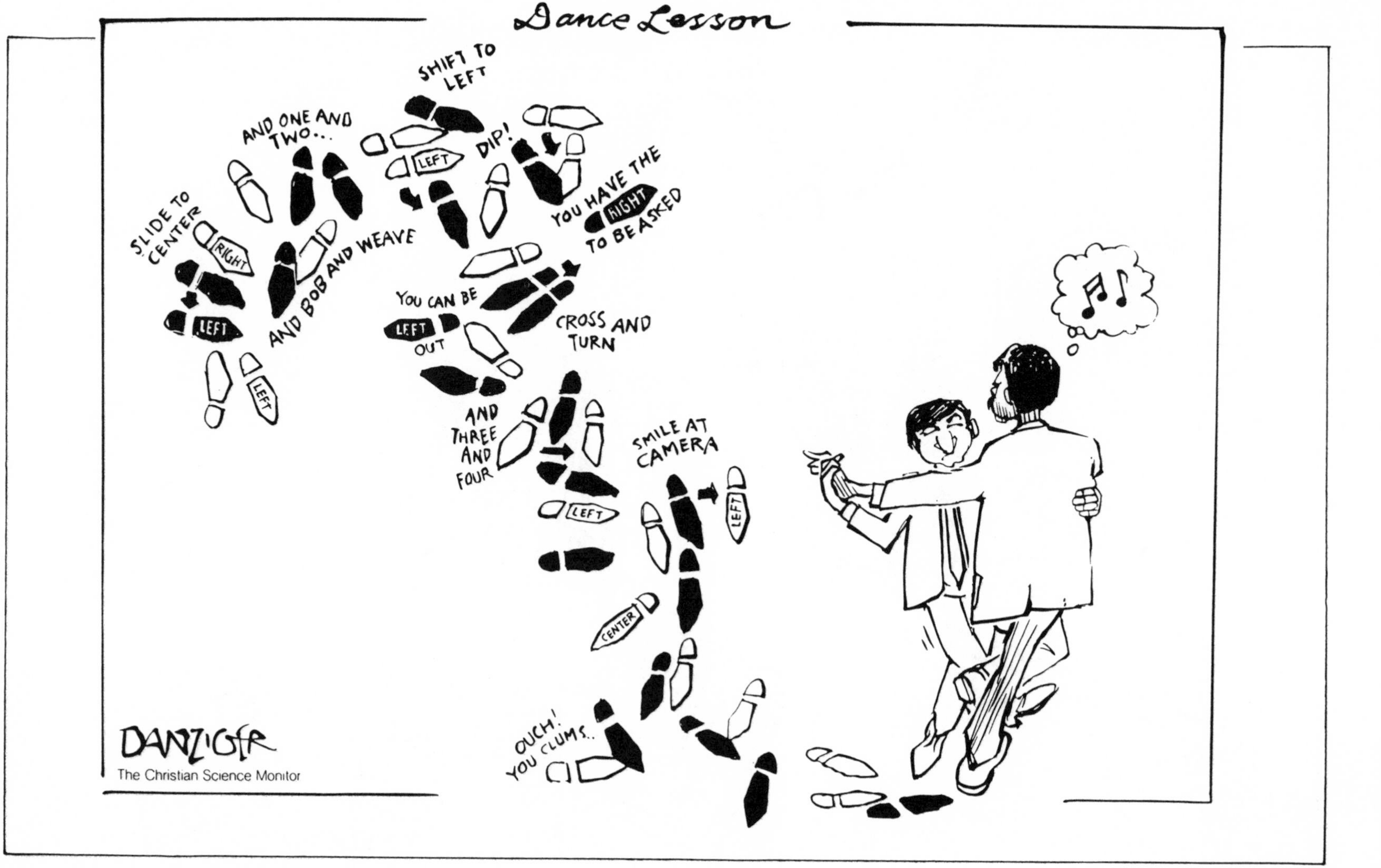
Dance Lesson
SLIDE TO CENTER
RIGHT
LEFT
LEFT
AND ONE AND TWO...
AND BOB AND WEAVE
SHIFT TO LEFT
LEFT
DIP!
YOU HAVE THE RIGHT TO BE ASKED
YOU CAN BE LEFT OUT
CROSS AND TURN
AND THREE AND FOUR
LEFT
SMILE AT CAMERA
LEFT
CENTER
OUCH! YOU CLUMS..
DANZIGER
The Christian Science Monitor

ATLANTA

DRIVER
DOES NOT
MAKE
CHANGE

DANZIGER

The Christian Science Monitor

The Bushes at Home
Reaching out to Black America, George and Barbara do research...

DANZIGER
The Christian Science Monitor

JAPAN

NEXT EXIT DETROIT

DANZIGER
The Christian Science Monitor

Over Tokyo...

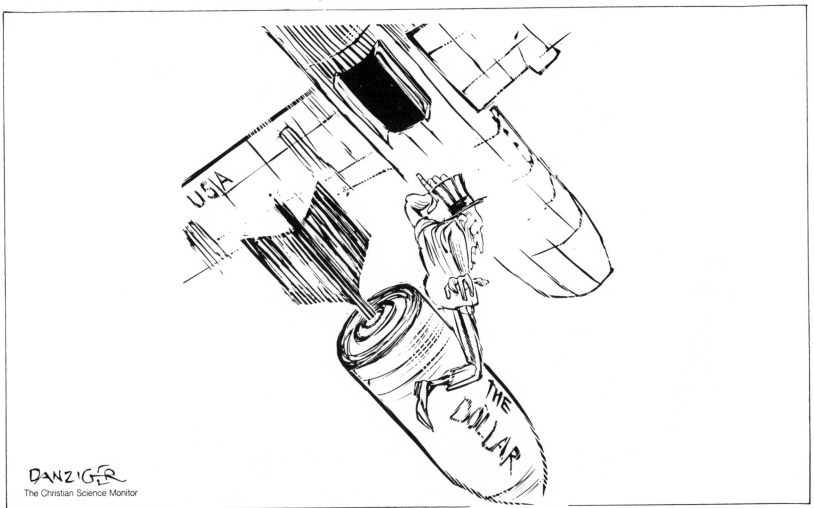

SO, WHEN the STEEL WORKERS LOST OUT TO OFFSHORE COMPETITION, I SAID, "WELL, THAT'S THE WAY THE FREE MARKET WORKS."

AND WHEN THE ELECTRONICS FIRMS CLOSED AND MOVED TO THE FAR EAST, I SAID, "THAT'S THE WAY MARKET FORCES HAPPEN SOMETIMES..."

AND WHEN THE AUTO FIRMS SHUT DOWN FACTORIES AND STARTED TO IMPORT, I SAID, "LET MARKET FORCES PREVAIL."

BUT... WHEN THE TEXTILE MILL OUTSIDE TOWN THREATENED TO CLOSE, I SAID, "ER... UM..."

"MAYBE, JUST MAYBE... THE GOVERNMENT SHOULD ACT TO STOP... Y'KNOW UNFAIR COMPETITION!

I MEAN... I WORK IN THAT MILL... ...AND I GOT PAYMENTS TO MAKE ON MY TOYOTA.

DANZIGER
The Christian Science Monitor

1987

DANZIGER

The Christian Science Monitor

PERFECT **LUGE** POSITION

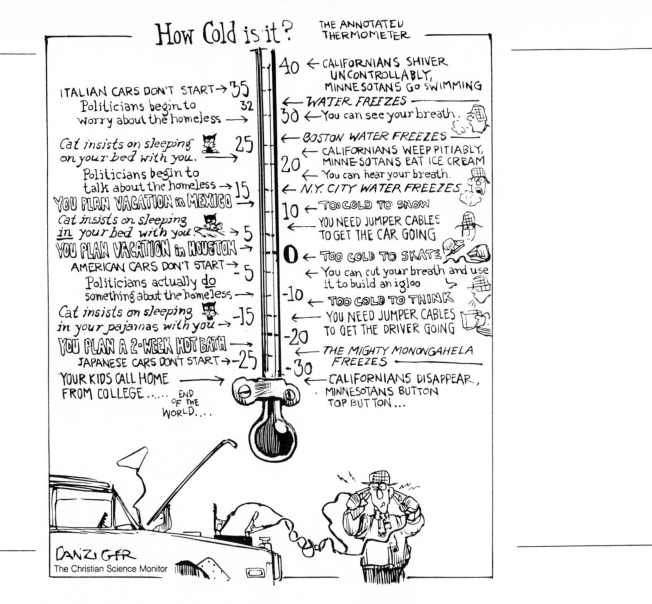

DANZIGER
The Christian Science Monitor

DANZIGER

The Christian Science Monitor

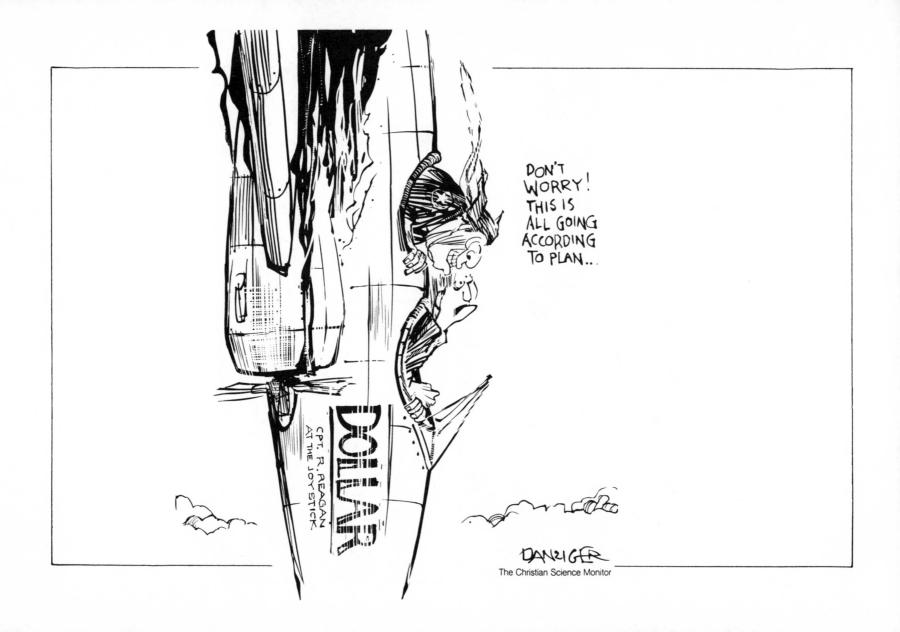

Sorry...

THERE WILL BE NO CARTOON TODAY. THE SIGNS WERE ALL
WRONG. VIRGO WAS ASCENDING. SAGITTARIUS WAS IN
THE THIRD HOUSE OF JUPITER. CAPRICORN IS IN THE POPPER.
TAURUS IS IN THE DRIVEWAY. BUT MAYBE TOMORROW...

DANZIGER
The Christian Science Monitor

OVERHEARD IN CONGRESS

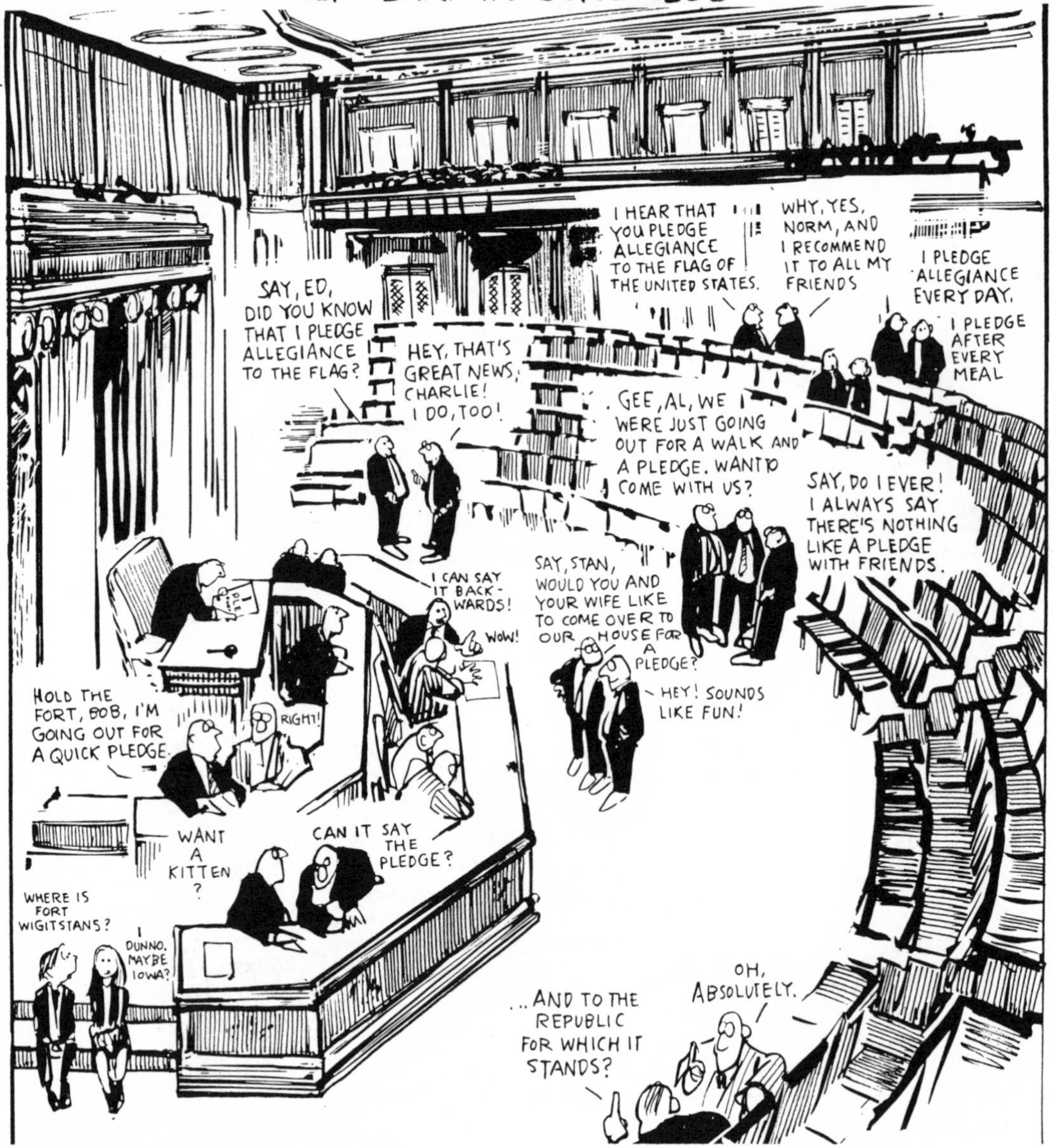

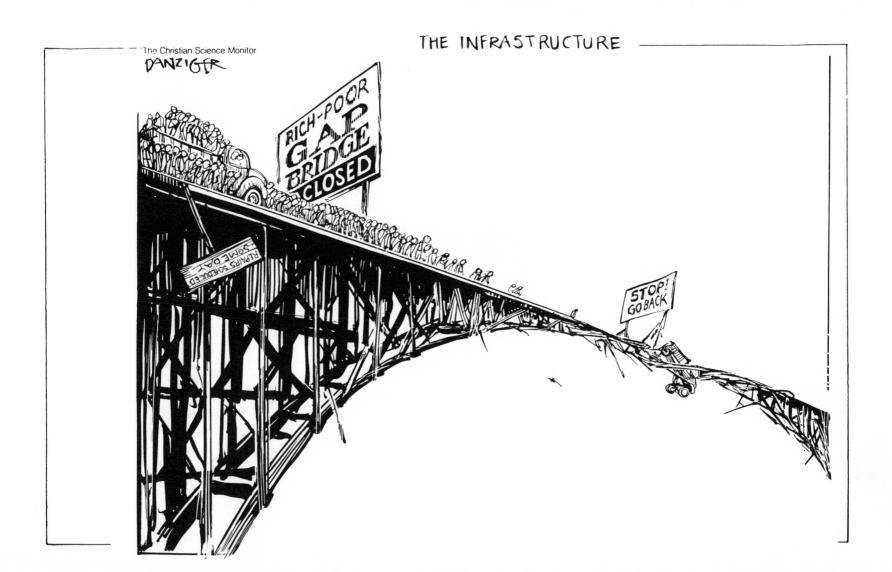

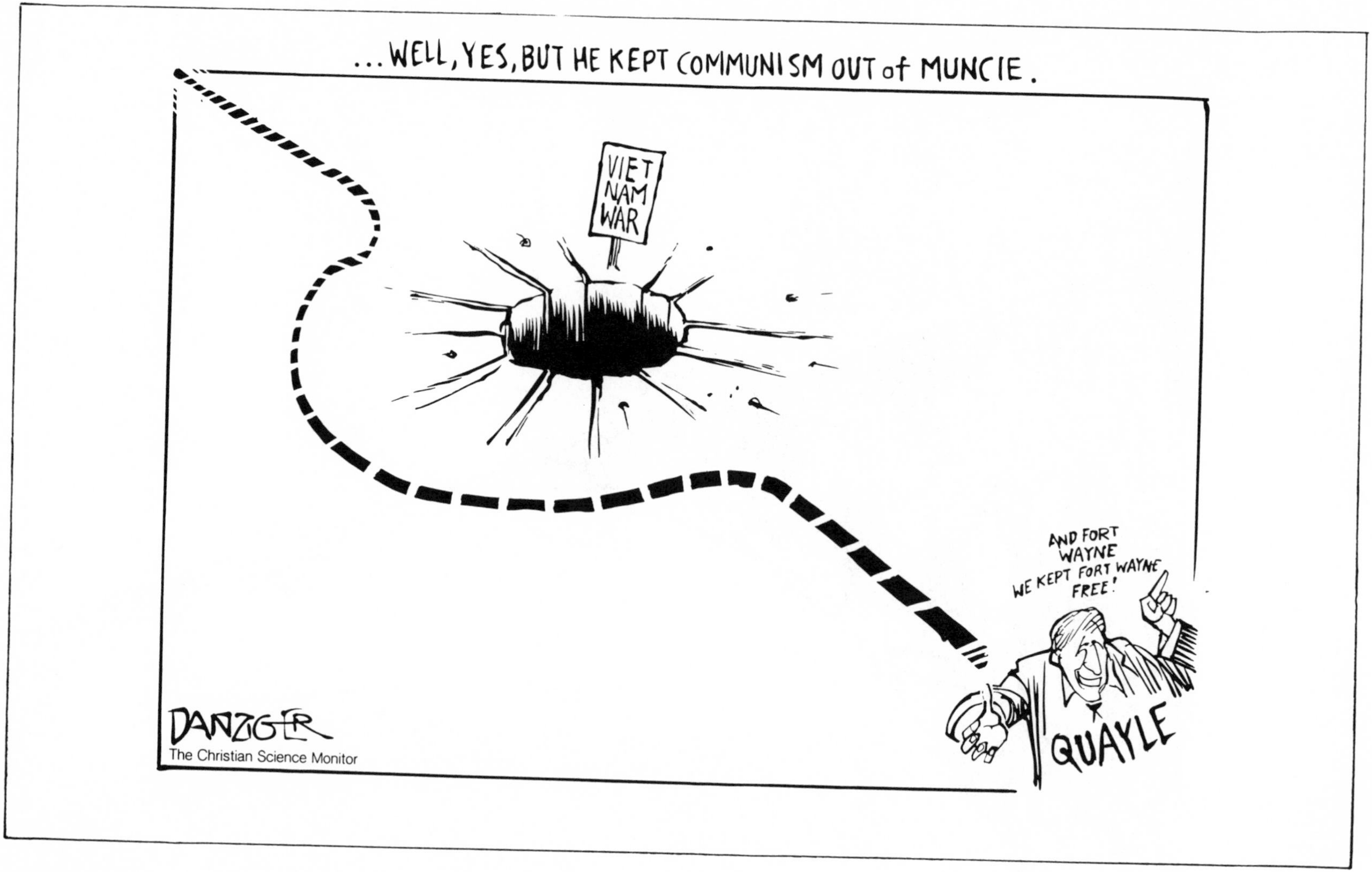
...WELL, YES, BUT HE KEPT COMMUNISM OUT of MUNCIE.
VIET NAM WAR
AND FORT WAYNE WE KEPT FORT WAYNE FREE!
QUAYLE
DANZIGER
The Christian Science Monitor

Back to School

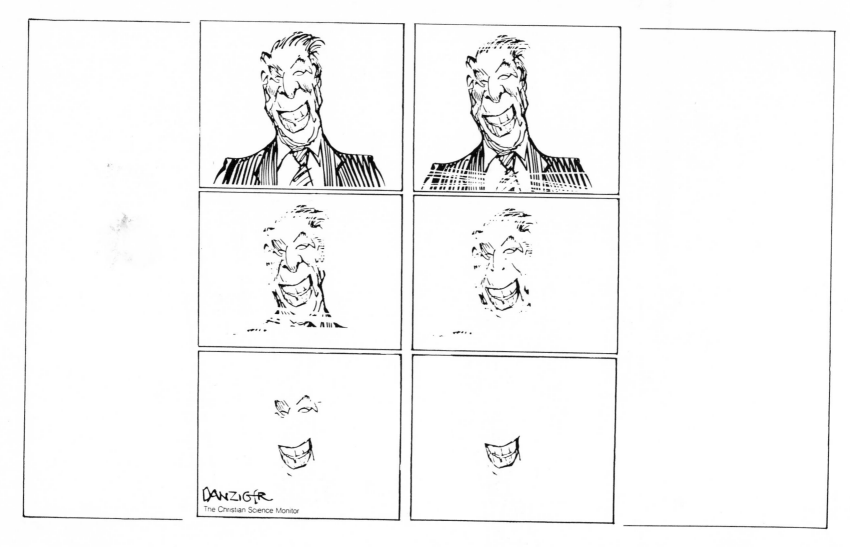

DANZIGER
The Christian Science Monitor